REBEL GIRLS

CELEBRATE PRIDE

25 TALES OF

SELF-LOVE AND COMMUNITY

Good Night Stories for Rebel Girls and Rebel Girls are registered trademarks.
Good Night Stories for Rebel Girls and all other Rebel Girls titles are available for bulk purchase for sale promotions, premiums, fundraising, and educational needs.
For details, write to sales@rebelgirls.com.

This is a work of creative nonfiction. It is a collection of heartwarming and thought-provoking stories inspired by the lives and adventures of 28 influential people.
It is not an encyclopedic account of the events and accomplishments of their lives.

Some of the artwork in this book has been previously published in the book *Good Night Stories for Rebel Girls: 100 Tales of Extraordinary Women.*

Text by Alexis Stratton, Jestine Ware, Shadae Mallory
Foreword by Elena Favilli
Art direction by Giulia Flamini
Cover illustrations by Annalisa Ventura
Graphic design by Kristen Brittain
Special thanks: Amy Pfister, Anthony Allen Ramos, Dana Levinson, Eliza Kirby, Grace Srinivasiah, Gwen Pointer, Jess Harriton, John McCourt, Lydia Edwards, Marina Asenjo, Maithy Vu, Meghan Bartley, Michon Vanderpoel, Rich Ferraro, Sarah Parvis

Library of Congress Control Number: 2022948163
Rebel Girls, Inc.
421 Elm Ave.
Larkspur, CA 94939

www.rebelgirls.com

Printed in Italy
10 9 8 7 6 5 4 3 2 1
ISBN: 978-1-953424-28-0

FSC
www.fsc.org
MIX
Paper | Supporting
responsible forestry
FSC™ C018179

CONTENTS

FOREWORD

Dear Rebels,

My elementary school years were a magical time, filled with adventure, friendships, and games. But in middle school, everything felt different. I became more serious, anxious, and lonely. I didn't feel comfortable in a body that was changing and turning me into a teenager. I felt disconnected from my classmates, who had been my closest friends until that point, and everyone seemed to be more confident than me.

More than anything, I could not understand why boys and girls were suddenly considered opposite teams. I had spent my childhood climbing trees, running in the olive groves, skateboarding, jumping in the river, and pretending to be Raphael from the Teenage Mutant Ninja Turtles. Why were all these things suddenly not considered appropriate for a girl?

Over and over again, I found myself making choices that were different from the girls around me. One cold winter day, I met my cousin Angelica at a Carnival parade, a celebration with costumes and masks. Waiting for me on our town's main street, she was wearing a look that was quite popular among teenagers at the time: blue hair, torn jeans, metal chains, military boots, and black makeup. Angelica was a perfect punk. I will never forget the look on her face when she saw me approaching, dressed like a . . . chicken! My mom took a picture of us, which has since become a family heirloom: Angelica looking perplexed, and me, smiling, proud of my white onesie with a tiny red crest on top.

I have a feeling that my confusion would have been much easier to navigate had I held a book like this in my hands. You see, what I didn't know at the time was that there is not just one way to be a girl, just as there is not one way to be a boy. I didn't know that the range of possibilities in front of me was much greater than the rigid, binary choice between male and female that seemed like the only option.

This book is a celebration of those possibilities. That's why it's called *Rebel Girls Celebrate Pride*. I am so proud of these stories because they show the power of love in all its forms. They will remind you that there is nothing wrong with who you are or who you want to be. Thankfully, lots has changed since I was a kid. Today, you have an entire vocabulary at your fingertips to describe the full spectrum of gender identity and sexual orientation. Whether you're gay, bisexual, asexual, heterosexual, transgender, pansexual, lesbian, queer, cisgender, or nonbinary, this book will remind you of the liberating power of love and acceptance.

You will read the story of Menaka Guruswamy and Arundhati Katju, who fought for years to overturn a law that discriminated against LGBTQ people in India. You will find out about Laverne Cox, who shattered Hollywood stereotypes and became the first openly trans woman to be nominated for an Emmy Award for acting. You will discover athletes who have broken all sorts of barriers in soccer, skateboarding, swimming, snowboarding, and tennis. All these stories prove that when freedom and love are protected, being happy becomes easier for everyone.

As you read about these intrepid trailblazers, remember that you too play an important role in preserving the rights that so many people before you have fought for. The respect you show to others, the causes you choose to defend, and the actions you take every day have an impact on making the world a better place. Let the stories in this book remind you that we all deserve to be loved and respected for who we truly are.

—Elena Favilli, Founder, Rebel Girls

SCAN TO HEAR MORE!

BONUS! AUDIO STORIES!

Download the Rebel Girls app to hear longer stories about some of the unstoppable musicians in this book. You will also unlock creative activities and discover stories of other trailblazing women. Whenever you come across a bookmark icon, just scan the code, and you'll be whisked away on an audio adventure.

ALANA SMITH

SKATEBOARDER

Alana was seven when their feet first touched a skateboard. As they swooshed through the quiet streets of their Arizona neighborhood, their heart took flight. They loved the feeling of wind whipping around them. They loved the board's sturdiness, and the whir of the wheels underneath.

Soon, Alana was taking lessons at a skateboarding school in town. Their pulse pounded each time they sped down the ramp or launched into the air. They rode down thin rails. They flipped their skateboard this way and that. They twisted their body mid-jump.

They fell—often. And sometimes it hurt. But each time, they got up, shook themself off, and skated on.

When Alana was 12, they flew to California to compete at a tournament. There, they tried a trick that no one competing in the women's category had ever done in a competition before: a 540 McTwist. To do a McTwist, Alana had to spin one and a half times in the air while holding the edge of their board with one hand.

The crowd applauded as Alana flew down the curve of the half-pipe. But they missed their landing and—*oof!*—skidded on the ground.

On Alana's next try, they sped down the half-pipe and up the other side. Suddenly, they were airborne—upside down and spinning. They grabbed the edge of their board like they'd practiced. Then, their wheels clacked hard against the ground. The audience cheered. Alana had landed it!

Alana came out as bisexual when they were 16, and right before competing in the Olympics in 2021, they told the world they were nonbinary. They said, "Going into the Olympics, I just wanted to be my authentic self."

BORN OCTOBER 20, 2000

UNITED STATES OF AMERICA

ILLUSTRATION BY
RUT PEDREÑO

"IF YOU LOVE
SOMETHING ENOUGH,
AND YOU PUT YOUR
MIND TO IT AND
YOU REALLY WORK
AS HARD AS YOU
HUMANLY CAN,
ANYTHING'S
POSSIBLE."
—ALANA SMITH

ALOK VAID-MENON

WRITER AND PERFORMANCE ARTIST

Alok was always fond of colors—the brighter, the better. When selecting clothes, they always chose vivid patterns. If the boys' clothes were too drab for Alok, they dressed in their mother's and sister's things. Alok didn't feel like a boy or a girl. As they grew up, Alok began to understand that "boy" and "girl" weren't the only options and that they were nonbinary. They began to use the pronouns "they" and "them."

Sometimes people were mean about the way Alok chose to dress, which made them sad and afraid. So Alok turned their feelings into art, performing onstage and writing beautiful poetry.

One day, a dress nearly leaped off the rack at Alok, begging to be worn. They put it on nervously.

But when Alok strolled down the street, they felt completely at peace. Vibrant material billowed around their legs. The breeze ruffled their long, flowy hair. They wore some purple lipstick and shiny shoes just for fun.

Once, someone stopped Alok at the grocery store and asked: "Why do you dress like that?"

Alok started to walk away, but the person admitted they used to like dresses too. They laughed it off, but the person seemed wistful, like they missed wearing dresses. *What if all clothes were for all people?* Alok wondered.

They knew exactly what to do. They started designing clothing that anyone could wear, no matter their gender. Alok's clothes feature the brilliant colors and patterns they have always loved.

Alok rocks their strong style every day. After all, fashion is for everyone.

BORN JULY 1, 1991

UNITED STATES OF AMERICA

ILLUSTRATION BY
PEARL AU-YEUNG

"BE YOURSELF UNTIL
YOU MAKE THEM
UNCOMFORTABLE."
—ALOK VAID-MENON

BELLE BROCKHOFF

SNOWBOARDER

Once upon a time, there was a girl who flew across the snow like magic. Even though Belle is from Australia, the driest continent in the world, she comes from a long line of snow athletes. Belle took to the slopes on skis at age three, and at age 10, she hopped on a snowboard.

Belle loved the cold rush of the wind against her face and the thrill of the steep mountain with its twists and turns. Her heart beat fast, and adrenaline coursed through her. She was one with her snowboard.

Belle started off competing in small contests in Australia. When she was 17, she signed up for larger international competitions. She finished 36th in her first World Cup championship. She kept trying, and two years later, she finished third. Belle was proud to be the first Australian woman to win a Snowboard World Cup medal.

Finally, Belle was ready for her first Olympics. It was in Sochi, Russia, where it's illegal to be openly part of the LGBTQ community. Belle was nervous, but she didn't want to hide her sexuality. Ahead of the games, she came out to reporters as a lesbian. They asked if she was scared to compete.

"I don't want to risk my safety," Belle said. "I want to be proud of who I am and be proud of all the work I've done."

In Sochi, she was interviewed for a documentary called *To Russia with Love*. She showed her anxiety, anger, and defiance about anti-LGBTQ laws in Russia and expressed her support and love for members of the LGBTQ community living there.

No matter where she goes, Belle will not compromise who she is.

BORN JANUARY 12, 1993

AUSTRALIA

"I OWE A LOT TO MY
SNOWBOARDING
BECAUSE THAT WAS THE
ONE THING THAT GAVE
ME A LOT OF PEACE AND
A LOT OF HAPPINESS."
—BELLE BROCKHOFF

BILLIE JEAN KING

TENNIS PLAYER

Once upon a time, there was a girl named Billie Jean who loved to throw and hit any ball that came her way. But it was the 1950s in California, and women weren't "supposed to" play sports. Still, Billie Jean's dad told her that girls could do whatever they put their minds to. And Billie Jean's mind was set on one thing: tennis.

After a few lessons at a local park, she told her parents: "I am going to be number one in the world."

She practiced every day and won her first tournament at 15. By her 20s, she was a world champion.

Some people *still* said women could never be as strong or smart as men. Former tennis champ Bobby Riggs insisted that men were better than women—and he challenged Billie Jean to a tennis match to prove it.

By now, it was 1973. Bobby was in his 50s and barely practiced. Billie Jean was 29 and one of the sport's top players.

If I win, she realized, *I could really help move things forward for women.*

So she accepted his challenge. When the big day came, more than 30,000 people filled the Houston Astrodome stadium, and more than 90 million people watched on television.

Bobby started off strong, but Billie Jean's power came through with each swing. Slowly, she wore Bobby down. Finally, Billie Jean hit one lightning-fast shot—and Bobby failed to return it.

Billie Jean won! She tossed her racket in the air as the crowd went wild.

Bobby and his fans said a woman could never defeat a man. In the Battle of the Sexes, Billie Jean proved them wrong.

Today, she and her wife, Ilana, run World TeamTennis, a professional tennis league where *everyone* plays together—no matter their gender.

BORN NOVEMBER 22, 1943

UNITED STATES OF AMERICA

ILLUSTRATION BY
EMMANUELLE WALKER

"GIRLS HAVE BEEN TAUGHT TO BE PERFECT, AND BOYS HAVE BEEN TAUGHT TO BE BRAVE. DON'T LET YOURSELF THINK THAT YOU HAVE TO BE PERFECT."
—BILLIE JEAN KING

CLARA BARKER

MATERIAL SCIENTIST

As a kid growing up in a working-class neighborhood, Clara knew she was different. She couldn't understand why everyone was telling her she was a boy when she knew she was really a girl.

In Manchester, England, in the 1980s and '90s, the world was different than it is today. Clara's TV had four channels, and there was no internet. And because of a law passed in 1988, British schools were banned from supporting and celebrating LGBTQ people.

Clara studied hard and became an engineer and a scientist. But she felt like she was drowning in sadness.

She had to make a change. In 13 years working in the sciences, Clara had only ever met two other scientists in the LGBTQ community, and neither was transgender. If Clara came out, she thought her career would be over.

Still, being who she was was important to her. Clara took a leap—and came out as a transgender woman.

Soon after, in 2015, she applied for a job as a laboratory manager at the University of Oxford. When Clara walked into her interview, she didn't look like a "typical scientist." She was trans. She had tattoos. And she was carrying a My Little Pony purse. Nervous, she sat down. The interviewers asked Clara about all the interesting work she had done. With confidence, she spoke about the ultrathin materials she works with—fascinating materials used in electronics, from touch screens to solar panels. Later, they offered her the job!

Clara was stunned. From then on, she made it her mission to show the world that it doesn't matter what you look like or where you come from. Clara knows that anyone who loves science can be a scientist.

BORN JANUARY 27, 1979

UNITED KINGDOM

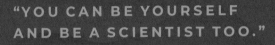

"YOU CAN BE YOURSELF
AND BE A SCIENTIST TOO."
—CLARA BARKER

ILLUSTRATION BY
OLIVIA M. HEALY

DARCIE LITTLE BADGER

EARTH SCIENTIST AND WRITER

When Darcie was little, her mom and her grandma Elatsoe told her stories passed down in their Lipan Apache tribe. Whether the tales were about ghosts, mosters, or animals, Darcie loved them all.

Darcie went to libraries and bookstores, eagerly looking for books about Lipan Apache people. She couldn't find a single one, so she decided to write one herself.

In first grade, Darcie wrote a 40-page book, and her father helped her submit it to a couple of publishers. She got her very first rejection letter a few weeks later. But Darcie was determined.

In college, Darcie applied for the creative writing program twice. Twice, she was rejected. She was disappointed. She always thought she'd study writing, become an author, and get published right away. Things weren't working out that way, though.

Instead, Darcie studied oceanography. She went on a research trip to Bermuda and rode a tiny boat far into the ocean. When she lowered herself into the cool water, she loved seeing the depths under her feet and wondered what lay in the shadows. Darcie was hooked!

Then, she combined her two loves: writing and science. She became an editor of scientific papers while writing novels on the side. She named her first book *Elatsoe*, after her grandmother. The main character, Ellie, is Lipan Apache and asexual, just like Darcie.

When *Elatsoe* was released, readers couldn't get enough of Ellie's adventures with her ghost dog, Kirby. Darcie felt proud that little Lipan Apache girls and asexual kids could finally see themselves represented on the shelves.

BORN 1987

UNITED STATES OF AMERICA AND LIPAN APACHE

"MY RESPONSIBILITY IS TO FIGHT FOR THE BEST VERSION OF THE FUTURE THAT I CAN."
—DARCIE LITTLE BADGER

ILLUSTRATION BY ILIANA GALVEZ

FIORE DE HENRIQUEZ

SCULPTOR

Although Fiore was born in Italy, a country known for marble statues made by masterful artists, she never once thought of becoming a sculptor—until, at 19, she first touched clay.

Fiore was helping a friend prepare a project in a studio at their university. As Fiore kneaded the clay with her long fingers, she became so hypnotized she almost fainted.

She looked into her hands and realized she was making a portrait—a sculpture of a person's face. The edges were rough, and some details were missing from the face. But as she gazed at her fingerprints on the clay, she knew she wanted to keep making her mark.

From then on, Fiore's one true love was sculpting. People marveled at the sculptures she made: a phoenix flying out of the ashes, a huge tree with eagle's feet, and so many portraits! Her sculptures looked like they could come to life in an instant. She could make eyes glint mischievously and hair look like it had been ruffled in the wind.

A lot of Fiore's sculptures showed pairs, and sometimes she talked about herself as being two people in one body. Fiore was raised as a girl, but she was actually intersex. As a teenager, she found out her body didn't fit doctors' typical definitions of "boy" or "girl." Fiore called herself lucky, though. The things that made her different made her unique.

Throughout Fiore's life, many famous people asked her to make portraits of them or their loved ones—including the Queen of England's mother, President John F. Kennedy, and even TV star and media mogul Oprah Winfrey. Wherever she went, Fiore proudly broke the mold—and refused to be anything but the fierce, creative human she was.

JUNE 20, 1921–JUNE 5, 2004

ITALY

18

"I CAN SEE BOTH SIDES
BECAUSE I AM BOTH SIDES."
—FIORE DE HENRIQUEZ

FISCHER WELLS

STUDENT ATHLETE AND ACTIVIST

Fischer never thought of herself as the sporty type. But in seventh grade, she told her parents she wanted to play field hockey. The problem was, there were only two other girls who wanted to play. So Fischer set about recruiting her friends. She asked them at lunch and in the hallways. Soon Fischer had enough people to make a whole team.

At practice, she dashed across the field. She liked the way her muscles burned as she ran. She enjoyed making her teammates laugh. And she loved the sharp crack her stick made when she whacked the ball.

But the day before her first game, Fischer's parents got a devastating call: Fischer couldn't play. Fischer is transgender, and school officials in Kentucky said trans girls couldn't play on girls' teams.

Fischer's insides felt like they would crumble. She wanted to cry. She wanted to scream! But Fischer's parents, teammates, and coach rallied around her, and they got Fischer back on the team. They didn't win a single game—but that didn't matter. For Fischer, it just felt great to play.

Then Fischer got more bad news. Lawmakers proposed a state law that would make it illegal for trans girls to play on girls' teams. It seemed targeted at Fischer—she was the only out trans girl playing middle school or high school sports in her whole state.

So Fischer mustered up all her courage and went to the state capitol to testify against the bill. Before a room of stern-faced state senators, she took a deep breath and told her story as cameras clicked around her.

Sadly, the lawmakers passed the law. But Fischer will keep fighting for her rights. If there's one thing that field hockey has taught her, it's *never give up*.

BIRTH DATE UNKNOWN
UNITED STATES OF AMERICA

OPPOS
SB83

ILLUSTRATION BY
JACKY SHERIDAN

"[PRIDE IS] AN
ENTIRE MONTH TO
CELEBRATE MYSELF."
—FISCHER WELLS

HANNAH GADSBY

COMEDIAN

SCAN TO HEAR MORE!

Once upon a time, there was a quiet child named Hannah who grew up in a small Australian town. Hannah was so quiet that when she did speak up, people had to lean in close to hear her.

She wasn't like other kids in her town. As a person on the autism spectrum, Hannah was often overwhelmed by crowds and noises. She had trouble making friends. When she closed her eyes, she imagined that she must be an alien—a strange being from another planet who was left on Earth to muddle through.

To make matters more complicated, as she got older, Hannah realized she was queer—and in her state, loving someone of the same gender was illegal.

Hannah had a hard time figuring out where she fit in. After studying art history in college, she worked at a bookshop, as a projectionist at a movie theater, and even as a farmhand!

But one thing Hannah always loved was making people laugh. One day, when she was 27, a friend encouraged her to enter a comedy competition in Melbourne—and she did. There, everyday people like Hannah stood on a big stage and told stories and jokes. When it was Hannah's turn, she stepped up to the microphone and took a deep breath. She told a story about her dog. The audience laughed at all the right places. Every time, Hannah's heart soared. She felt more at home onstage than she did anywhere else.

Hannah became a comedian, and eventually, she told her stories on stages around the world. It is still scary sometimes to let her voice be heard. But whenever she gets nervous today, her wife looks her in the eyes and says, "Don't panic. Who do you want to be?"

And Hannah? She just wants to be Hannah.

BORN JANUARY 12, 1978

AUSTRALIA

"THE POWER OF A JOKE IS NOT IN THE WRITING. IT IS HOW YOU WRAP YOUR VOICE AROUND IT."
—HANNAH GADSBY

ILLUSTRATION BY SHELBY CRISWELL

IREEN WÜST

SPEED SKATER

When Ireen was 10, she begged her father for a pair of speed skates. She lived in the Netherlands, where speed skating first started—way back in the 13th century. Eventually, her father gave in.

Ireen and her dad crunched across the snow to a frozen canal nearby. Her eyes widened as she watched skaters sweep across the ice. She slid her feet into her skates, laced them up, took a deep breath, and stepped forward.

She felt the smooth surface beneath her blades, marveling at the magical way she glided, one skate at a time. The wind nipped at her cheeks and nose—but she loved every minute of it. That day, Ireen and her father skated 12 miles! When they got home, Ireen's muscles ached. But all she wanted to do was get back out there.

So she did—again and again. Soon, Ireen was whizzing in big loops around rinks like a race car on skates, leaving her competitors far behind.

Ireen trained nonstop and eventually joined a professional team. She won her first Olympic gold medal in 2006 when she was 19—and competed at four more Olympic Games after that.

At the Beijing Olympics in 2022, Ireen was 35 years old. People said she was too old to win. But that only made her work harder. Her first event was the 1,500-meter race. When the starting gun fired, Ireen shot forward. She flew around each curve. Faster and faster she went until, finally, she blazed across the finish line—setting a new Olympic record.

With that win, Ireen became the oldest speed skater to win gold and one of the most decorated LGBTQ Olympians of all time. Shortly after, she got engaged to fellow speed skater Letitia de Jong. Together, the two glided off to new adventures.

BORN APRIL 1, 1986

NETHERLANDS

"I ENJOY THE CHALLENGE TO PERFECT [MY SKATING] AND KEEP BREAKING NEW BARRIERS. I HAVE YET TO SKATE THE PERFECT RACE."
—IREEN WÜST

ILLUSTRATION BY T.L. LUKE

JANELLE MONÁE

SINGER, SONGWRITER, ACTOR, AND AUTHOR

Once upon a time, there was a child named Janelle who loved singing to a crowd. It didn't matter where—at church, in talent shows, or in school plays—Janelle was happiest when they were performing.

After high school, Janelle decided to study music and theater in New York City. But the giant city seemed stifling. Janelle spent most of their time working, at school, or in their tiny apartment. The gigs Janelle booked had them singing tired old songs. Janelle felt bored and boxed in. They wanted to be original, and that meant writing and performing their own music.

Janelle packed their bags and left for Atlanta. Immediately, they knew they'd found the right place. There were so many talented Black artists, and the city was alive with all kinds of music—rap, hip-hop, soul, and more. Best of all, people wanted to hear Janelle's songs.

To make some money, Janelle had a job at an office-supply shop. One day, they used a store computer to respond to a message from a fan who had seen them sing. Their boss was not happy, and Janelle was fired. Instead of looking for another job they found boring, though, Janelle decided to aim big. They put everything they had into making a career as a performer.

With their focus on their art, Janelle became a huge star. They could create freely, just as they had always wanted. Janelle wrote and sang about gender, love, and the future. They mixed sounds and types of music in a new and electrifying way. Later, they acted in movies and TV shows and wrote a book.

Journalists were always curious about Janelle's sexuality and gender. Eventually, Janelle came out as nonbinary and pansexual, which means they are attracted to people of all genders. "I know who I am," they said. "I've been playing a version of some parts of me, but now I'm owning all of me."

BORN DECEMBER 1, 1985
UNITED STATES OF AMERICA

"I FEEL MY FEMININE
ENERGY, MY MASCULINE
ENERGY, AND ENERGY I
CAN'T EVEN EXPLAIN."
—JANELLE MONÁE

LAUREN ESPOSITO

ARACHNOLOGIST

Lauren started collecting insects when she was very young. She loved flipping over rocks behind her house in Texas to discover what squirming, wriggling creatures were hidden underneath. Once, she even turned over her mother's flowerpots in search of crickets. But her mother, a biologist, didn't mind. When Lauren came inside the house with a beetle or a moth cupped in her hands, her mom taught her how to keep her specimens safe in glass jars and egg cartons.

When Lauren grew up, she found a new group of creepy-crawlies to study: arachnids!

Arachnids, such as spiders and scorpions, are eight-legged animals. Scorpions had scared Lauren when she was little, but she later realized that they are super cool. Scorpions are ancient. The oldest scorpion fossils are 450 million years old. Scorpions are mysterious. They glow under ultraviolet (UV) light—but no one really knows why. And scorpions are unique. They are the only arachnids that give birth to live young.

Lauren wanted to discover new scorpion species and teach people about these amazing animals. Armed with a UV light, a net, and some test tubes, Lauren tramped through forests, beaches, and deserts from Malaysia to Mexico, collecting specimens. Back in her lab in California, she studied them under microscopes and told the world what she found.

Even though Lauren was queer, she didn't know any other LGBTQ scientists in her field. So in 2018, she launched the 500 Queer Scientists campaign to help LGBTQ scientists feel seen, heard, and supported. At first, Lauren's goal was to find 500 scientists who could share their stories. By 2022, 1,800 scientists had joined her online community!

BORN NOVEMBER 29, 1981

UNITED STATES OF AMERICA

"VISIBILITY . . . IS IMPORTANT FOR MENTAL HEALTH, FOR STANDING UP TO INJUSTICES, AND FOR MENTORING CURRENT COLLEAGUES AND FUTURE SCIENTISTS."
—LAUREN ESPOSITO

ILLUSTRATION BY MAJU BENGEL

LAVERNE COX

ACTOR AND ACTIVIST

SCAN TO HEAR MORE!

Whenever she stepped onto the stage, with bright lights above her and the audience rustling in front of her, Laverne was filled with joy. She knew she was where she belonged. For her, that feeling was special and rare. Laverne was assigned male at birth. But inside, she knew she was a girl.

All through elementary, middle, and high school, Laverne adored dance—tap, jazz, and especially ballet. She pirouetted and leaped across the stage, rehearsing until everything was perfect. But in college, she discovered another way to perform that she loved even more: acting. She acted in small films and onstage in New York City. At the same time, slowly but surely, Laverne began to live authentically. She came out as transgender.

Laverne accepted herself. *But will Hollywood accept me?* she wondered.

One day, she saw a TV show with a character played by an openly transgender actor. Laverne couldn't look away. She wanted to be on that screen—and for the first time, she felt like she could. The next day, she printed postcards to send to agents and casting directors with her photo and the statement: "Laverne Cox is the answer to all your acting needs."

Her big break came a few years later when she was cast on a hit TV show set in a women's prison. She played Sophia, a kind but complicated transgender hairdresser who faced challenges with strength. The role earned Laverne an Emmy nomination—a first for an openly trans woman.

Laverne wants everybody to experience the belonging she felt the first time she danced onstage. "If someone needs to express their gender in a way that is different, that is okay," she says. "That's what people need to understand, that it's okay."

BORN MAY 29, 1972
UNITED STATES OF AMERICA

ILLUSTRATION BY
MIA SAINE

"I WAS TOLD MANY TIMES THAT I WOULDN'T BE ABLE TO HAVE A MAINSTREAM CAREER AS AN ACTOR BECAUSE I'M TRANS, BECAUSE I'M BLACK, AND HERE I AM . . . AND IT FEELS REALLY GOOD."
—LAVERNE COX

MARSHA P. JOHNSON & SYLVIA RIVERA

ACTIVISTS

Best friends Sylvia and Marsha often walked through New York City together. They especially loved the artsy West Village neighborhood. But they began to notice something: there were a lot of people sleeping on park benches and in alleys. Many were young people who were part of the LGBTQ community. Sylvia and Marsha had to help.

Both Sylvia and Marsha were transgender—and proud of it! Sylvia was young and spirited, and always called out injustice. Marsha was older and brought her sweetness and big smile wherever she went. Their common goal of helping young people united them.

Slyvia and Marsha knew what it was like to be without a place to stay. They'd both left home when they were very young. And they knew there were thousands more queer kids just like them who ran away because their families didn't accept them. Many shelters were religious and didn't accept gay or trans kids. There was nowhere else for them to go.

One day, Marsha had an idea. *Let's rent a hotel room so these kids can have a safe place to rest*, she said.

And that's what they did—over and over again. One of them went to pay the front desk for two rooms while the other snuck dozens of kids inside.

Over time, Marsha and Sylvia scraped the money together to rent a four-bedroom apartment. It didn't have heat or electricity, but it was safe. They made it comfortable and welcoming, and named it STAR House.

This was the first safe haven for transgender youth in New York City. Because of Marsha's and Sylvia's big hearts and trailblazing ideas, there are now many organizations that serve trans people.

MARSHA, AUGUST 24, 1945–JULY 6, 1992
SYLVIA, JULY 2, 1951–FEBRUARY 19, 2002
UNITED STATES OF AMERICA

"IF YOU WANT GAY RIGHTS, YOU'RE GOING TO HAVE TO FIGHT FOR IT. AND YOU'RE GOING TO HAVE TO FIGHT UNTIL YOU WIN."
—SYLVIA RIVERA

ILLUSTRATION BY GGGGRIMES

MENAKA GURUSWAMY & ARUNDHATI KATJU

LAWYERS

O nce upon a time, there were two women who fought for what was fair. Menaka and Arundhati both started studying the law in India. Later, they studied at universities around the world.

Everywhere they went, they noticed *lots* of laws that discriminated against LGBTQ people. Some laws wouldn't let LGBTQ people live together, get married, or adopt a child. Some laws made it so transgender people couldn't express themselves. Some countries even threw people in jail or killed them just for being who they were.

Menaka and Arundhati started defending people who were called criminals for being members of the LGBTQ community. In 2011, Arundhati opened her own law office. In 2013, she and Menaka fought against an anti-LGBTQ law in India and lost. But they didn't let that disappointment get them down. They continued working, studying cases and crafting new, clever arguments. In 2015, they tried a case for a transgender person. This time, they won!

Now they felt ready to tackle the anti-LGBTQ law in India again. Could they really overturn a 157-year-old rule? It seemed impossible, but they decided to take on the law anyway.

They brought students, celebrities, and citizens of every age and all different walks of life to the court to show how the law harmed the community. The judges listened carefully. After considering Menaka and Arundhati's arguments, the court overturned the unjust law.

A few hours after the decision, the monsoon rains came. "It's quite lovely," Menaka said. "The skies have opened up to celebrate with us."

MENAKA, BORN NOVEMBER 27, 1974
ARUNDHATI, BORN AUGUST 19, 1982
INDIA

"SO MUCH OF WHY I LOVE THE LAW IS THAT . . . YOU CAN USE YOUR COUNTRY'S CONSTITUTION TO EXPAND FREEDOM."
—MENAKA GURUSWAMY

ILLUSTRATION BY
CARLA BERROCAL

MOJI & MARGARET SOLAR-WILSON

ENTREPRENEURS

When Moji and Margaret, both Nigerian immigrants, fell in love, they wanted to show their commitment to each other by getting married. They were living in New York City, but they decided they would travel back to Nigeria for their wedding. A traditional African ceremony was exactly what they envisioned. They wanted bright colors and bold patterns, spicy foods, drummers, dancers, and a ceremony to honor their ancestors. They wanted it all.

They had a problem, though. All their plans were canceled as soon as vendors discovered they were a same-sex couple. In Nigeria and many other countries in Africa, it was illegal to be lesbian. If they ever returned home, they could be imprisoned for 14 years.

Moji and Margaret got married in the US with the help of their friends. They are the first-known Nigerian lesbian couple to be legally married in America. But even in New York City, some people in the immigrant community were not supportive. Moji and Margaret started thinking about moving away and starting fresh. But where would they go? They were homesick for Nigeria, yet they couldn't return there.

What if we could bring home to us? Moji and Margaret thought.

As they talked with each other, an idea started to take shape. The couple bought 40 acres of land in Texas and created a resort inspired by African villages. They called it Solar-Wilson Village.

Moji and Margaret have now hosted hundreds of gatherings, weddings, and celebrations. They host people of all ethnicities, genders, sexualities, and religions. They are proud to have built a place where all are welcome.

MOJI, BIRTH DATE UNKNOWN
MARGARET, BIRTH DATE UNKNOWN
NIGERIA AND UNITED STATES OF AMERICA

ILLUSTRATION BY
EMILY THOMAS

"[WE] CREATE
SAFE SPACES
FOR CELEBRATION,
RELAXATION, OR
RECHARGING."
—MOJI & MARGARET
SOLAR-WILSON

MOLLY PINTA

ACTIVIST

When Molly came out to her parents as bisexual at age 11, she felt lucky that they responded with love. Molly knew that not every kid had that. Many of her LGBTQ classmates worried that people would treat them differently if they came out. She wished she could help—but she was only out to her family.

When Molly and her mom marched in a Pride parade in Aurora, Illinois, near their village of Buffalo Grove, Molly felt surrounded by love and acceptance. Balloons, streamers, and rainbow flags filled the air as the crowd joyfully made its way through town. People congratulated her on her sign, which said she had started her school's Gay-Straight Alliance club and was 12, out, and proud. Molly wanted every teen to feel as accepted as she did that day. As she and her mom drove home, Molly wondered aloud, *What if Buffalo Grove had a Pride parade?*

With her parents' help, Molly made a video. Sitting in front of a Pride flag with rainbow colors in her hair, Molly came out to the whole world. And she told people about her dream of bringing Pride to her small hometown.

Donations poured in, and friends lined up to volunteer. Molly also got some mean letters from people who thought Buffalo Grove was no place for Pride. It was scary that some of her neighbors judged Molly without even knowing her. But she brushed off the haters and kept working.

Finally, the big day came. In June 2019, 2,000 people walked and danced and waved their signs in Buffalo Grove's very first Pride parade—and 8,000 more showed up to watch. It was an enormous success!

The Pinta family's organization, the Pinta Pride Project, now hosts yearly parades, an LGBTQ prom, support groups, and much, much more.

BORN 2006

UNITED STATES OF AMERICA

"I'M NOT BEING BRAVE,
I'M JUST BEING ME."
—MOLLY PINTA

ILLUSTRATION BY
LILIA MICELI

PATRICIA CAMPOS DOMÉNECH

NAVAL AVIATOR AND SOCCER COACH

Once upon a time, a girl named Patricia dreamed of soaring above the clouds. Patricia grew up in a small village in Castellón, Spain—a land of sweet oranges and green mountains. Above those mountains, planes sometimes flew in smooth arcs through the bright-blue sky. She longed to be up there too.

I want to be a pilot, she declared.

The townspeople couldn't believe their ears. *Girls can't be pilots!* they said.

Patricia had heard this a lot. She loved playing the trumpet, but people told her, *That's a boy's instrument!* And when she kicked around a soccer ball, her grandma scolded her, saying, *Act more ladylike!*

But Patricia kept practicing the trumpet. She kept playing soccer. And she kept her eyes on the skies. When she was 24, she joined the navy, where she would learn to be a pilot.

Patricia put on her new uniform with pride and headed to the navy base. She trained until her whole body ached. Sometimes, male soldiers said mean things about women and gay people, which made Patricia angry. Most didn't know Patricia was a lesbian.

On the day of her first flight, as she taxied down the runway's dark surface, she remembered watching jetliners above the mountains. Her plane gathered speed. Patricia felt her back pressing against her seat. She pulled on the control stick. Her heart leaped as she shot into the sky.

Eventually, Patricia became Spain's first female fighter pilot. She didn't come out until after she left the military, and even then, some of her old colleagues did not support her. But when Patricia told the world who she was, she felt as free as a plane soaring across the clouds.

BORN MARCH 12, 1977

SPAIN

"I THINK WHEN A WOMAN OPENS A DOOR, YOU OPEN IT FOR ALL OTHER WOMEN."
—PATRICIA CAMPOS DOMÉNECH

ILLUSTRATION BY INGRID SKÅRE

PATRICIA VELÁSQUEZ

ACTOR AND MODEL

Patricia sat on her mother's couch. She could smell delicious cooking coming from the kitchen and hear the crackle of fireworks outside. But all she could focus on was her mom sitting beside her.

Patricia had acted in movies and TV shows and modeled all over the world, but she always felt like she was hiding something. She was a lesbian, and at the time, it wasn't common to see queer celebrities being their authentic selves in the limelight. When she was finally ready to tell her friends and family, she thought deeply about what it would mean.

In her mom's living room, Patricia took a deep breath and said, "Mama, it's true. I am gay." Patrica couldn't believe she had actually said the words. Silence filled the room, and Patricia was nervous as tears filled her mother's eyes. Her mom usually didn't show big emotions. But then she took Patricia's hand and said, "I'm here for you, and I love you." Patricia was overjoyed. She knew it was hard for her mother to understand, and yet she could feel her mom's love and support in every word. Finally, Patricia felt free to be herself.

As a member of the Wayuu people, an Indigenous tribe native to Latin America, Patricia also felt strongly about helping her community. She created a charity organization called the Wayuu Taya Foundation. It helps improve living conditions for the Wayuu and create access to education.

Patricia kept acting, modeling, and helping others after she told her mom she was gay. Later, she came out to the rest of the world in her book. Patricia is proud of all parts of her identity. She says, "My life feels authentic and unburdened now."

BORN JANUARY 31, 1971

VENEZUELA

ILLUSTRATION BY
MANUELA CUNHA SOARES

"THE BIGGEST EXAMPLE I WANT TO
GIVE TO MY DAUGHTER WHEN SHE GROWS
UP IS TO BE STRONG, TO COME OUT OF
ADVERSITY, TO BE PROUD OF WHO SHE IS
AND TO NEVER DENY WHO SHE IS."
—PATRICIA VELÁSQUEZ

PHYLL OPOKU-GYIMAH

ACTIVIST

Once upon a time, there was a girl who was always looking up at the night sky. Her name was Phyllis, Phyll for short.

Phyll's grandmother would watch her as she gazed at the stars. *Our ancestors are up there in those stars,* she would say. *They are always guiding us through tough times.* Phyll never forgot her magical words.

In high school, Phyll became interested in politics and activism. She was starting to realize that she was part of the vibrant LGBTQ community. She noticed that articles, books, and events like Pride parades mostly highlighted white people.

What about people who look like me? Phyll wondered.

She sifted through articles and books about queer history. Phyll learned about people like Sylvia Rivera, Marsha P. Johnson, and Audre Lorde. She felt excited by the Pride celebrations for people of color they had inspired. But those celebrations took place in America, far from Phyll's home in England.

Just like she did as a little girl, she looked up at the night sky and thought about a solution. *What would* my *Pride look like?* Phyll asked herself.

With the help of her friends, Phyll cofounded a celebration called UK Black Pride, the first of its kind in all of Europe. It is a day when LGBTQ people of color can come together to joyfully celebrate one another. They sing, dance, give speeches, and show up for their community.

Phyll protests anti-LGBTQ laws and builds UK Black Pride to be bigger and better each year. And even now, when she's thinking about a tough problem, Phyll looks to her ancestors in the sky. They can always help her find the answer.

BORN NOVEMBER 20, 1974
UNITED KINGDOM

"I'M A DESCENDANT OF WOMEN WHO FOUGHT BACK, WHO LOVED, AND WHO SPOKE THE TRUTH."
—PHYLL OPOKU-GYIMAH

ILLUSTRATION BY DANIELLE ARRINGTON

QUINN

SOCCER PLAYER

What do you want to be when you grow up? Quinn's first-grade teacher asked their class.

Quinn's eyes lit up. They knew *exactly* what they wanted to be. They pursed their lips together as their crayon swept across their paper. Slowly, Quinn's picture became clear: a blond-haired, blue-eyed person stood on an Olympic podium wearing a shiny gold medal around their neck.

Which sport was being celebrated was anyone's guess. Quinn's parents drove them and their sisters all over Toronto—to hockey practice, ski lessons, and swim team.

But most of all, Quinn loved soccer. Quinn dribbled down the field, dodged between orange cones, and slammed the ball into the goal. They came home sweaty and exhausted. But they never gave up.

Finally, when they were 18, they made Canada's national soccer team. They were thrilled!

In 2021, Quinn and their teammates flew to Tokyo, Japan, to compete in the Olympic Games. Canada played hard every match, and they made their way to the top. Finally, in their last game, Canada beat Sweden in a high-stakes shoot-out. Quinn and their teammates rushed onto the field, cheering and hugging one another.

Not only did Canada's women's soccer team win gold for the very first time, but Quinn made history too—as the first out trans and nonbinary medalist in the Olympics.

When an official placed the medal around Quinn's neck, they remembered the picture they'd drawn in first grade. They looked at their teammates, who had helped them reach this magical day, and smiled. They couldn't stop smiling if they tried.

BORN AUGUST 11, 1995

CANADA

46

"SOCCER IS SUCH A JOY IN MY LIFE, AND I HOPE THAT PEOPLE SEE THEY CAN BE THEMSELVES AND CONTINUE TO PLAY SPORTS AND THERE'S A PLACE FOR THEM."
—QUINN

ILLUSTRATION BY
BETSY FALCO

SHERENTÉ

DANCER AND ACTIVIST

Once upon a time, a vibrant teenager named Sherenté put on a colorful shawl and began to dance. They stepped and twirled to the beat of a drum. To some, it looked like a familiar ceremonial dance. But it wasn't. It was a groundbreaking, life-affirming performance.

As a citizen of the Narragansett tribe, Sherenté spent their childhood watching their elders dance in ceremonies called powwows. At powwows, people wear special outfits and honor their ancestors' traditions. Sherenté's father performed in Eastern War Dances, and their mother danced Fancy Shawl. At first, Sherenté danced the same style as their father, but it didn't feel right. They were more comfortable performing with the women. Sherenté was Two-Spirit. LGBTQ indigenous people use this term to refer to people with genders that stretch beyond the categories of "male" or "female."

A lot of the dances at powwows are competitions. When Sherenté started Fancy Shawl dancing, some powwow officials were so upset that they told the judges not to score Sherenté's dances. Since Sherenté was Two-Spirit, some people thought they shouldn't be allowed to compete. For over a year, the judges refused to score them. Sherenté felt sad and isolated, but they persevered. Allies protested to help Sherenté. Together, they reminded their community that acceptance was their traditional way. Finally, Sherenté's dances were scored, and eventually, they placed first!

In college, Sherenté was involved in activism. They wanted to create positive change and raise awareness of the hardships Two-Spirit people face. Their work got Sherenté a lot of attention. Soon, a documentary, *Being Thunder,* was made about Sherenté, and they could share their journey with the world.

As Sherenté says, "No one can tell our stories better than us."

BORN JUNE 11, 2000

UNITED STATES OF AMERICA AND NARRAGANSETT

48

ILLUSTRATION BY
AMY PHELPS

"PRIDE IS NOT ABOUT BEING
ACCEPTED; IT'S ABOUT ACCEPTING
YOURSELF REGARDLESS OF OTHER
PEOPLE'S OPINIONS."
—SHERENTÉ

SCAN TO HEAR MORE!

THERESA GOH

PARALYMPIC SWIMMER

Theresa smiled as she slid into the plastic pool float. She pulled her arms through the water, moving herself across the pool. Her legs floated behind her like a mermaid tail. Theresa was born with a condition called spina bifida that left her paralyzed from the waist down, and when she wasn't splashing around in the pool, she used a wheelchair.

As she got older, Theresa spent hours mastering butterfly, freestyle, backstroke, and her favorite stroke of all—breastrstroke. Some mornings she wanted to snuggle under warm covers, but she still got up early to lift weights and swim. When she lost a race, she'd cry big tears. But she always got back in the pool.

When Theresa was a teenager, she had a crush on a girl in her class. Singapore, where she lives, was not friendly toward LGBTQ people. So Theresa focused on swimming and didn't tell anyone how she felt. Her parents could tell something was up, though. One day, her mom said: "You know Daddy and I just want you to find somebody who will love you and take care of you, and it doesn't matter if it's a boy or girl."

Theresa hugged her parents tight. Her family accepted her sexuality, but she was afraid to tell anyone else. In some of the countries where she competed, you could even be put in jail for being gay.

After winning a bronze medal at the Paralympic Games in Rio, Theresa decided to tell the world who she was. She came out as a lesbian in a national paper. She was nervous to go to practice the next day. When she got there, though, people told her how happy they were for her. They were proud of her. And Theresa was proud of herself.

BORN FEBRUARY 16, 1987

SINGAPORE

"BE KIND, BE BRAVE, BE YOURSELF."
—THERESA GOH

ILLUSTRATION BY ANNIE LIU

WILL LARKINS

ACTIVIST

Will's first protest was in second grade. They didn't like their cafeteria food, so they grabbed construction paper and markers and scribbled out a petition demanding change. Then, they passed it around for their classmates to sign.

It wasn't just Will's activism that made them stand out, though. Will wanted to play with dolls, spin around in gowns, and drape themself in sparkling necklaces. But everyone said, *Boys don't do that!*

Lying in bed at night, they wondered, *Is there no one like me out there?*

But then, in seventh grade, they made a new friend at camp who said there were tons of people like Will. They weren't alone after all. Will learned all they could about LGBTQ people. They were so excited they finally had words to describe themself.

I'm gay, they said. And, later, *I'm nonbinary*—which means their gender doesn't fit easily into the categories of "boy" or "girl."

By the time Will started high school, they knew they weren't broken. And whenever people tried to say LGBTQ people were, Will spoke out.

In 2022, when lawmakers in Florida tried to pass a law that stopped teachers from talking about LGBTQ people, Will traveled to the state capitol. Standing tall before a roomful of legislators in Tallahassee, they told their story and urged the lawmakers to support LGBTQ students.

Unfortunately, the law passed—but Will kept fighting. They organized protests and registered voters. Once, wearing a vibrant red gown, they taught their class about the Stonewall riots, an important moment in LGBTQ history.

No matter what the world says, Will wants all LGBTQ kids to know this: "You are not alone, you were never alone, and you will never be alone."

BIRTH DATE UNKNOWN
UNITED STATES OF AMERICA

ILLUSTRATION BY
IZZY EVANS

"WE WILL NOT
BE SILENCED."
—WILL LARKINS

X GONZÁLEZ

ACTIVIST

X stood in front of the microphone, the hot Florida sun beating down. Emotion swelled within them as they looked out at the gathered crowd. They took a deep breath and began to speak.

Just three days earlier, X had been in the school auditorium when an alarm had gone off. Something terrible was happening. X huddled between cold metal chairs with their teachers and fellow students.

Later, X found out that a student with a gun had killed 17 students and teachers, and injured 17 more.

School no longer felt like a safe place for X. They and their friends stayed together, not wanting to eat, sleep, or even shower. But soon, X found their voice and gave their first speech against gun violence.

Some adults scoffed at the speech, saying that X didn't understand the issues. But X had thought it through. They knew that stricter and safer policies around guns could make a difference and save lives. Around the country and around the world, people heard X's call to action.

Together with their friends and classmates, X organized a huge protest called March for Our Lives. Hundreds of thousands of people marched together to support gun reform. X gave another powerful speech. And soon after, Florida passed a bill that made it harder for people in the state to get their hands on guns.

The new bill was a big victory for X and their friends, but there were more battles on the horizon. Later, leaders in Florida passed laws that hurt gay and transgender students. X, who is bisexual and nonbinary, raised their voice once again. Sometimes they feel frustrated about all that needs to be done. But they keep speaking out, fighting to create a safer world for everyone.

BORN NOVEMBER 11, 1999
UNITED STATES OF AMERICA

"FIGHT FOR YOUR LIVES
BEFORE IT'S SOMEONE
ELSE'S JOB."
—X GONZÁLEZ

WRITE YOUR STORY

DRAW YOUR PORTRAIT

KEEP CELEBRATING!

FLY YOUR FLAG

The LGBTQ community is represented by the Progress Pride flag.
Can you design a flag that represents you?

1. Brainstorm. Think about the colors, symbols, and images that describe who you are as a person. Maybe you love the beach, so your background color is the deep blue of the ocean. Maybe you love to read, so your central symbol is a book. Let your imagination run wild!
2. On a big sheet of paper, use markers, crayons, or colored pencils to design your flag.
3. Hang it up in your room or wherever you'd like to see it every day.

SING IT LOUD AND PROUD

Janelle Monáe loves expressing themself through music.
Make a playlist that shows the world who you are.

1. Choose songs that describe your mood or feelings. They might have lyrics you relate to or a beat that makes you instantly get on your feet and start moving—no matter who is watching. Maybe you just really look up to the singer and want to be like them when you grow up.
2. Next time you need a confidence boost, blast your playlist and sing or dance in front of the mirror.

DREAM DINNER

You've learned about some truly inspiring people in this book. What would it be like to spend some time with them?

1. Pick two or three people you've read about and imagine what it would be like to have a meal with them. Where would you go? Where would you sit? What would you eat? What would you talk about?
2. If you'd like, imagine adding some characters from books, TV, movies, or even real life to the mix. What might the star of your favorite TV show say to Sherenté Harris? What would the main character of the last book you read share with Theresa Goh?
3. Write a story about this dream dinner and share it with a friend.

IT'S TIME TO CELEBRATE

Activists like Molly Pinta and Phyll Opoku-Gyimah have created Pride events in their communities. If you got to plan your own celebration, what would it look like?

1. Think of festivities you'd like to see in your town or city—it could be in honor of Pride or something else.
2. Write a description of some of the events you could organize. It could be a parade, a concert, a dance party, a rally for an important cause—the sky's the limit.
3. Think of a few people you'd ask to participate in your event. They could be celebrities or people in your community you admire.
4. Once you have a vision for your celebration, design a flier advertising some of the amazing events you've come up with.

SCULPT A SELF-PORTRAIT

Fiore de Henriquez created beautiful sculptures that captured the spirits of her subjects. Would you like to sculpt a self-portrait that shows the world who you are?

1. Gather some materials to make your sculpture. You can use clay like Fiore did, if you have it, but you can also use folded paper, cardboard, clean recyclables, or any other supplies you have on hand. Make sure to ask an adult for help setting up, especially if you're using messy materials like paint or glue.
2. Sketch your sculpture first. You can try to make it look just like you, or you can take a more abstract approach.
3. Start sculpting!
4. When you're finished, write a description of your sculpture—like the ones that hang in museums.

TERMS TO KNOW

We use a wonderfully wide range of words to describe gender and sexuality. Here's a helpful guide to the difference between gender identity, gender expression, and sexual orientation. If you have questions, talk to a parent or a grown-up you trust!

GENDER IDENTITY

Gender identity is your inner knowledge of your own gender. Everyone has one. For some people, their gender identity matches the sex they were assigned at birth—that is, what's on their birth certificate. For other people, it does not match. People with that experience may call themselves "transgender." Most people have a gender identity of man or woman (or boy or girl). For other people, their gender identity does not fit neatly into one of those two genders. They may use the word "nonbinary" or another word to describe their gender. Gender identity is not visible to others. You can't look at someone and "see" their gender identity.

GENDER EXPRESSION

We use gender expression to feel comfortable with ourselves and to show information about our gender to others. Some forms of gender expression are names, pronouns, clothing, makeup, and hairstyle. Two words we often use to describe gender expression are "masculine" and "feminine." A masculine-presenting person might wear a suit to a fancy party, while a feminine-presenting person might wear a dress. Words like "gender nonconforming" and "androgynous" may be used to describe gender expressions that are not traditionally masculine or feminine—maybe they go to the party wearing a bow tie and high heels. What is considered masculine or feminine changes over time and varies from place to place. (For example, in some cultures, men wear long hair as a sign of masculinity.)

SEXUAL ORIENTATION

Sexual orientation describes a person's attraction to another person. That attraction may be physical, romantic, or emotional. People use many different words to describe their sexual orientation, including "straight," "lesbian," "gay," "bisexual," "queer," and "asexual."

You can't tell what someone's sexual orientation is just by looking at them, or just based on their gender identity or gender expression. It's possible to know who you are attracted to before you start to date. For some people, it may take time to be sure about their sexual orientation.

ABOUT GLAAD

GLAAD rewrites the script for LGBTQ acceptance. As a dynamic media force, GLAAD tackles tough issues to shape the narrative and provoke dialogue that leads to cultural change. GLAAD protects all that has been accomplished and creates a world where everyone can live the life they love. Visit www.glaad.org to learn more.

MORE STORIES!

For more stories about amazing women and girls, check out other Rebel Girls books.

LISTEN TO MORE EMPOWERING STORIES ON THE REBEL GIRLS APP!

Download the app to listen to beloved Rebel Girls stories, as well as brand-new tales of extraordinary women. Filled with the adventures and accomplishments of women from around the world and throughout history, the Rebel Girls app is designed to entertain, inspire, and build confidence in listeners everywhere.

THE ILLUSTRATORS

Twenty-five extraordinary female and nonbinary artists from all over the world illustrated the portraits in this book. Here are their names.

ALICE NEEDHAM-PEARMAIN, **UK**, 19

AMY PHELPS, **USA**, 49

ANNIE LIU, **USA**, 51

BETSY FALCO, **UK**, 47

CARLA BERROCAL, **SPAIN**, 35

DANIELLE ARRINGTON, **USA**, 45

EMILY THOMAS, **UK**, 37

EMMANUELLE WALKER, **CANADA**, 13

EVE ARCHER, **UK**, 27

GGGGRIMES, **USA**, 33

ILIANA GALVEZ, **USA**, 17

INGRID SKÅRE, **BRAZIL**, 41

IZZY EVANS, **UK**, 53

JACKY SHERIDAN, **NORTHERN IRELAND**, 21

K. WROTEN, **USA**, 11

LILIA MICELI, **ITALY**, 39

MAJU BENGEL, **BRAZIL**, 29

MANUELA CUNHA SOARES, **BRAZIL**, 43

MIA SAINE, **USA**, 31

OLIVIA M. HEALY, **UK**, 15

PEARL AU-YEUNG, **USA**, 9

RUT PEDREÑO, **SPAIN**, 7

SOLENE CHAUDOIS, **FRANCE**, 55

SHELBY CRISWELL, **USA**, 23

T.L. LUKE, **USA**, 25

ABOUT REBEL GIRLS

REBEL GIRLS is a global, multi-platform empowerment brand dedicated to helping raise the most inspired and confident generation of girls through content, experiences, products, and community. Originating from an international best-selling children's book, Rebel Girls amplifies stories of real-life women throughout history, geography, and field of excellence. With a growing community of nearly 20 million self-identified Rebel Girls spanning more than 100 countries, the brand engages with Generation Alpha through its book series, award-winning podcast, events, and merchandise. With the 2021 launch of the Rebel Girls app, the company has created a flagship destination for girls to explore a wondrous world filled with inspiring true stories of extraordinary women.

As a B corp, we're part of a global community of businesses that meets high standards.

Join the Rebel Girls community:
- ✦ Facebook: facebook.com/rebelgirls
- ✦ Instagram: @rebelgirls
- ✦ Twitter: @rebelgirlsbook
- ✦ TikTok: @rebelgirlsbook
- ✦ Web: rebelgirls.com
- ✦ Podcast: rebelgirls.com/podcast
- ✦ App: rebelgirls.com/app

If you liked this book, please take a moment to review it wherever you prefer!